Boosted: The Vital Credit, Budget & Financial Improver How-To Manual for Normal People

Boosted: The Vital Credit, Budget & Financial Improver How-To Manual for Normal People

A.K. Armstrong

YOUR PERSONAL CREDIT

Dedication

This book is sincerely dedicated to those who possess a strong desire to improve their credit, budget, and finances. The reality is our credit is our representative. In many ways our credit informs others how to perceive us, without knowing who we are on a personal level. So, what does your credit currently say about you? Let us deep dive and cause our credit representative to represent us in a positive manner.

Table of Contents

INTRODUCTION

Your credit history is a great blessing to have. Some people take it for granted until it's too late and have ruined their good credit, and people generally find out They've ruined their good credit when they least expect it. No one is planning to ruin their credit. Still, we know there are credit repair services and options that will help you improve a horrible credit situation and escape bad credit. This is where credit repair aid can be handy, and in exchange, your credit score can represent if you take it upon yourself to fix your credit. On that basis, there are several credit forms available to you inside the credit repair program to help customers correct their credit history.

There are random situations that could occur and have an impact on your credit. As an example, you may have had a family emergency, which may have taken you away from work and as a result, you were unable to pay your bills on time, resulting in consumer agencies reporting your delinquencies. Let's say you pull your credit report and see that there are flaws that need to be contested based on the details you've researched. Whatever the situation that put you in the financial position you're in right now, please don't let your credit go down the toilet. The most important thing is to try to get your credit scores where you want them, and it all starts with the credit report and how to address inaccuracies and items that you may take issue with. To restore your credit to good standing, you need to have a strong desire to boost your credit rating. Having your life back in order should be your top priority. You don't need to consult with local credit repair agencies to get your credit to a desirable score. By following some strategies to be discussed in this book, you will learn how to lower your finance charges or even remove them altogether if you make the payments as agreed in the payment arrangement.

You can also assess online credit repair assistance where you can accept the option of receiving assistance from the comfort of your home. It would help if you use a bit of caution when accessing the online credit repair website, but you can make a point of testing the website's credibility. There are many websites out there that are bogus and would require you to pass on your payment information for them to pay your bills for you, and although that sounds nice, you need to make sure that credit repair letters sent on your behalf justify this complete settlement. It would be best to be confident that the corporation is lawful and manages what they claim will be done on your behalf. So, please be cautious in that regard.

Everyone needs a little help now and then. Needing credit repair is nothing to feel bad about because repairing your credit is a significant problem and shouldn't be treated as a failure or something that should cause personal embarrassment. Your credit is genuinely valuable; you need to take good care of it and thoroughly clean up your credit history to fix anything unfavourable on your report. If you notice that you're having financial problems, then pursue credit rehabilitation to help you get back on your feet again and you may also use the sample letters found within the Appendix as a guide to work to repair your credit independently.

You will learn how to set up a budget that can also help you catch up with the bills behind you while keeping up with the daily bills you have to keep on going down the road of optimistic credit repair. You'll discover that you should develop a strategy, and in time you'll find that your credit issues start to change and that your credit score will rise with time. Debt is something that most people on this planet must deal with. I would recommend that you attempt to fix your credit and avoid filing for bankruptcy, unless necessary (Bankruptcy: seek professional guidance from a lawyer if you are considering this option). Good credit scores can be achieved with the right credit services. Try not to cause your credit score to fall to the Poor category.

Good credit scores can be realized if you make a point of having the right plan of attack, if you will. Just bear in mind that there are so many programs out there that can support you with personal credit repairs. Poor credit is not a hopeless situation to get out of the situation, but make sure you get the necessary credit repair plan of action to boost your credit history.

When Does Credit Begin to Play A Role in Our Lives?

If you're applying for an apartment, applying for loans (home/auto/student) and applying for utilities in your name are some examples of when credit will play a role in your life. Please keep in mind, if you are already struggling to make debt repayments, or if you have struggled in the past, not only will your finances be hit, but so will your credit rating.

How Does Credit Negatively and Positively Impact Our Lives?

Credit plays a critical and constructive role, such as:

➢ Appropriate credit allows people from all walks of life to set up their businesses, raise their income, and support their families.

➢ For some people, the loan helps develop their houses and get relief from the monthly rent.

➢ At the same time, to others, it helps a lot in raising their standards.

The first thing you must do when you find bad credit is avoid panicking. With our very dicey financial practices, it is no wonder that more and more people are registered as bad debtors. Poor credit is not a joke, but it's not anything to complain over either. Many people assume that poor credit is a disadvantage in hunting for personal loans; this is somewhat true. However, lenders are continually providing poor credit personal loans and finding new tools to create borrowers' options. So, remain optimistic.

The purpose of this book is to provide rudimentary to more advanced information related to credit, while providing the purpose of credit and how credit is considered. This book contains information that should help those who are establishing credit for the first time and those who may have some financial challenges and wish to challenge inaccurate information that's on their credit report. I am confident that by the time you complete this book, you will be better equipped to improve your financial situation and can help others do the same.

CHAPTER 1: The Importance of Credit

A healthy credit score will make a difference for you. Your credit score will impact so many things like a car loan, car insurance, home loan, credit card interest and financing fees, work application, and more. Many employers use the credit score to determine among many eligible applicants. Your credit score also affects your loans in terms of lending interest rates, which will save a lot of money, particularly on a mortgage. (Leonard and Lamb, 2002)

Is Credit Considered When Applying for A Job?

When you attend a job interview, you expect to be asked about your credentials and job experience, but you certainly don't expect to be asked about your credit unless you apply for a place in the finance sector. A study by the Society for Human Resources Management reveals that about half of all employers carry out credit checks on work candidates as a normal part of the recruiting process.

Strong credit demonstrates more than good debt management skills, but it shows that you are a responsible person. If you have a bad credit history, this will serve as a red flag for employers-especially if your credit check shows up in collection accounts.

What Is A Credit Report? Who Needs It, and Why?

Most people seem to have no idea what a credit report is and how it would benefit them. A credit report is a report that outlines your credit history that can be accessed by businesses that consider extending credit products or services to you, such as loans, credit cards, or even phone contracts.

A credit report essentially contains complete records of all transactions made by you, including any expenditures or any payments made by you to the organization concerned. A credit report also contains your full identity, including your name, personal address, job status, and your social security number. Said report also includes credit applications, loans sanctioned by you, loans you have applied for but not issued to you, and credit that you still must pay. Also, a credit report also provides the monthly payments you are currently making.

You may still be thinking, "Why do I need a credit report?" and "Who is it that wants to see my credit report?" The answer is, perhaps someone you're trying to get a loan from. Banks and other financial institutions would probably order a credit report to see whether you can be trusted with a loan to buy a house, a car, renting an apartment, and applying for a job. Remember, credit is a numerical reflection of you.

The report will inform individuals of all the credit cards you have, any balances due, when the payments were made on time, as well as when the payments were made late. If you have ever been penalized for a late payment, such as having collection agencies contact you, this report also provides this detail. The report also states whether you've demanded credit, so any lender or creditor can see if you've been applying for a lot of credit lately or not. This knowledge helps lenders decide whether you can be trusted to repay borrowed money or loans.

Several firms compile credit reports, and each of them use many different sources to understand the credit history. Basically, that means that the higher the credit score, the more likely you will access credit-based services, and the cheaper such services would be.

If you apply for a loan of some kind, how do you think the lender would judge you? The lender reviews your credit report, which reflects on your credit history along with your credit score. The interest rate determined by the lender to lend you money is also decided based on your previous financial transactions, which are reflected in your credit report. Getting a poor credit report and credit score can be a good reason for others not to trust you for financial dealings.

When is Credit Checked and Why?

When you request a new loan or turn to a new supplier, they will review the loan against you to make sure you are on the right plan, which equates to the best interest rate for you as well. It is necessary that the lender carries out a credit check for those on monthly payment plans such as auto loans and mortgages.

The Three Credit Bureaus and Why the Credit Scores Vary for Each Credit Bureau.

Credit Reporting Agencies (CRA), collect and retain consumer credit information. The United States big three (3) CRAs are Equifax, Experian, and TransUnion, all publicly listed, for-profit firms. Each of those has many scores associated with them and used for a wide variety of products. The two most widely used strategies are Fair Isaac (FICO) score and bankruptcy score, the FICO score being the more prevalent of both. The FICO score has various official names. The Experian / Fair Isaac risk model (these people are known for their math, not their creativity), for TransUnion, is the Empirica, for Equifax the Beacon. While they are different models developed for different

CRAs, they are designed to predict the same outcomes. That is, if the same issuers, etc. report to the same offices, a 660 Empirica score can predict the same result as a 660 Beacon score.

Fair Isaac (FICO) people use several factors collected from the credit bureau to determine their ratings. For example, the Empirica model has 30 active factors available for use. If you get a score from one of the credit bureaus, you can see the four factors that affected the score most negatively for that person. Even those with decent grades would have the most damaging factors. They'll be in sequence from the most negative. That's important to know. Just look at the factors, and you will have your reason. You may not always agree with it, but you will have your explanation.

Your credit report will often show multiple scores, which represent different bureaus, and each can provide a different score. First, with your report in hand electronically or hardcopy, review the details displayed to determine why there is a difference in scores. Perhaps a creditor only reported to Experian, for example. Then use the score of the Bureau that had more relevant or detailed information. So again, if the report with the lower score had its first creditor information listed as 'serious delinquency' and the report with the higher score didn't confirm the same 'serious delinquency', not only was said delinquency only reported to one Bureau, but that's one less bureau that contains derogatory information, which can be a good thing.

Why Do Creditors Not Report to All Three Bureaus?

Why isn't every creditor reporting your history to all three credit offices? That's because every time your creditors send data about their experience with you to the Bureau, they pay a fee. Bottom line, some lenders don't think it's worth the cost. Before approving your loan or credit card application, creditors can request a credit report to save as much as possible.

Can One Boost Their Credit Score?

Do you know you can raise your credit score? Strategies to boost low credit score eludes many people. The first step in enhancing your credit is figuring out what your credit score is now. Each credit bureau provides one (1) free credit report per year. Additionally, if a user establishes an online account with each bureau, they can look at their score often for free. Order your report from all three credit reporting agencies. Often lenders or creditors report to one or two of the three, but one report can have negative marks, over the others.

Once you have access to your credit reports (electronic or hardcopy), you will have a clear picture of where you stand as it relates to your credit report. You may also identify the fundamental causes of your low ranking. The most popular negative items on a credit report include getting too much debt, collecting outstanding bills, financial problems like bankruptcy, not getting a long enough credit history, or submitting past debts to a collection agency.

How Do You Boost Your Credit Score?

Based on your issue set, you can derive a strategy to improve your credit score. Generally, you can get it done by yourself by establishing a personal plan based on your situation. As you determine your action plan, consider which factors most damage your credit. You can boost your credit score by:

1. Establish a FREE online account via each credit bureau in efforts to receive your credit report at no cost.

2. Access and review your credit report.

3. Locate all the items that you would like to dispute, items that are inaccurate (your current mailing

address, your name as it's displayed on your driver's license, incorrect phone numbers).

4. Use the corresponding letter within the appendix to dispute items listed in the above step 3 and contact each bureau accordingly.

Equifax Boost

Your Equifax credit score is important. It can impact the interest rate you receive on your mortgage, the credit cards you qualify for and even whether or not you can sign a lease without a co-signer.

Track Your Credit Score

First, check what type of credit score you have through the MyFICO site, which shows all 28 variations of the FICO credit score.

If you sign up for regular monitoring, you'll receive an updated score once a month.

Seeing your latest credit score will help keep you on the right track.

Make Payments on Time

An on-time payment history accounts for 35% of your FICO credit score. Your score will increase if you pay your bills on time but missing even one payment could cause a significant dip.

Lower Your Credit Card Utilization

If you have credit cards, check that your utilization percentage is lower than 30%. This percentage is calculated by dividing the current balance by the original credit limit. Said utilization percentage can also be found via Experian's site, for example. If your current balance is $300 and the credit limit is $1,500, your utilization percentage is 20%.

Keep Old Accounts Open

The average age of your credit history makes up 10% of your FICO score. Closing accounts could decrease your credit score. Every time you close an old account, you risk lowering the average age, as well.

Keep credit cards open if possible and avoid closing any credit cards unless there's a steep annual fee.

Get a Credit Builder Loan

Unlike regular lending products, credit builder loans are solely designed to help consumers improve their credit. Here's how they work.

The consumer in question applies for a credit builder loan from a reputable company like Self, which does not conduct a credit check.

The individual starts making regular monthly payments to Self, which keeps the payments in a secure account.

After the loan term is over, the consumer receives their money back, minus some fees. By this point, they should have a solid credit score.

TransUnion Boost

Maybe credit problems from your past haunt your current score. That's ok because you always have the power to change your credit habits.

You can boost or increase your credit score with TransUnion by utilizing their online dispute option as well. Remember to dispute information that is inaccurately placed on your report. The removal of said inaccuracies, should help to boost your score. Don't forget, there are sample letters found within the Appendix section to serve as a guide to removing unwanted items and boosting your score as well.

Good Credit Practices

Pay bills on time: Even if you cannot pay in full, be sure to make the minimum payment.

Watch your credit card balances: Make sure you're not using too much of your available credit.

Don't mindlessly open new credit card accounts: If you apply for new cards, make sure you don't do so too frequently. This behavior may look irresponsible to creditors.

Alert banks and card companies when you move: You don't want to see your bills have gone unpaid because the mail didn't go to the correct address.

Check your accounts online: There's no reason to wait for the bills to come in the mail. You should make sure payments are clearing and cards are being kept current.

Pay off delinquent bills: Paying down delinquent accounts won't remove missed payments from your report. But it can make you look better to creditors.

Look for inaccuracies: Sometimes information reported to the credit reporting agencies isn't quite right or is incomplete. The credit reporting agencies make it easy for you to dispute these inaccuracies. And remember, credit bureaus are just the messengers—it's up to you to let them know one of your creditors reported inaccurate information.

Experian Boost

Experian Boost lets you add on-time telecom and utility payments to your credit report, which could lead to a hike in your FICO ® Score. It's free, but it will only affect your Experian credit report and your FICO Score 8, one of several credit scores lenders may look at, depending on the loan you're seeking. The average Experian Boost user sees a 13-point increase in their credit scores.

Boosting your credit score via Experian's website can occur within minutes. Here's what I will recommend you do now if you'd like to see a potential credit score increase. I followed the below steps and received a 20-point increase (20 points can be the difference between a poor credit score to a fair credit score, it could be the difference between how much auto or mortgage logan you can receive. Believe me, 13 – 20 points is a big deal) within roughly 3 minutes, however, the average increase is 13 points:

1. Accessed Experian.com
2. Established a FREE account (no upgrades needed) and logged in.
3. By clicking the word Experian via the upper left corner of the screen, you're taken to the home page.
4. From the home page, scroll down to the section of the page that references Experian Boost, or via the very bottom of the screen, underneath Tools, click Experian Boost.
5. Add each of your accounts such as your energy bill, mobile phone / telephone bill, internet bill and water bill.

6. Now, you will have to include the account details that you use to pay said bills. In my case, once I selected my bank, I had to provide my bank account number and a password. Here's the deal, please – please DO NOT provide your actual login password, instead, access your bank account online (not via a mobile app) and via the locate temporary passwords. Once I logged into my online banking account, I clicked the Security link, scrolled down to the Manage Limited Access Passwords. So, via your online banking account (meaning accessing your bank account online), look for your Limited Passwords section.

7. Establish the limited password, copy and paste said temporary password into the Experian site and submit those details. Within minutes, you'll receive feedback and a credit increase if you have been paying previously mentioned bills with this newly added bank account. NOTE: You can add multiple bank accounts.

Your credit score, calculated from your credit report's information, is a measure of your creditworthiness, how good a risk you are to a credit granter. A large proportion of borrowers who can't qualify for a mortgage would be eligible if their credit scores were higher.

It accounts for around a third of your credit score and most situations. Loans and creditors use history to forecast potential expenses. Suppose you have a history of late payments and overload to persuade a lender that this activity won't continue. This is why your score is so important. Unfortunately, what's in the past is in the past and cannot be changed, so all you can do now is turn it around and start paying your bills on time.

How much debt you owe at the moment is also around one-third of your ranking. If you have loads of debt lenders, they will assume you are overextending yourself financially and that you are possibly having trouble repaying debts.

You can raise your score by paying as much of your existing debt as you can as quickly as possible, I recommend 25 days or sooner. For instance, if you spend $500 via credit card, attempt to repay that $500 within 25 days. Basically, each time that you spend, pay it off! If you do this, you will most certainly see an increase in your credit score. I check my credit via my online credit bureau account at least once or twice a week, consider it habit.

In my view, you should find a fast solution that will improve your reputation and help you apply for loans within 90 days. How?

You could write a dispute letter. Find enclosed in the appendix several dispute letters you could model. The first step you should take is to contact your credit bureau and request a dispute on your credit report's different entries. If the entries are disputable, the information is deleted, and your credit score gets a raise.

However, if the credit bureau cannot validate the details, the same will be automatically excluded. The moment your credit history eliminates derogatory information, you'll immediately enjoy a significant boost in your ratings.

This removal should be more than enough to get you back to affordable loans. You don't have to use a specialist credit restoration provider. You can actually do it yourself.

How to Increase your Credit Score by 100+ Points

Financial lenders already started tightening the gap on who they lend money to. If you're looking to purchase a new home, car, or some other big-ticket item soon, you'll undoubtedly want to make sure your credit score is good enough to attract lenders' approval. If your credit score drags, you will enjoy this method of improving it quickly.

Do you know the secret of improving your credit score lies within your credit report? Unfortunately, several people are ignorant of some credit reporting errors in their credit reports that significantly decrease their FICO score. Credit bureau reports errors like late payments, non-payments, written off accounts, settled accounts, old mobile phone accounts, and everything else conceivable, which obviously can drag your FICO score below what you thought possible.

The first thing you need to do is get your credit report copy. You'll want to do a summary of the report's details. These details will tell you precisely what makes up your credit report and your FICO score.

One thing I've learned, when you see it, most people know a mistake. Once you have found the report's flaws, you can potentially challenge them with the credit office and have it withdrawn within 30 days of filing. This you can do by writing a dispute letter listing the items and the anomalies you identified in your credit report.

You can raise your credit score by as much as 100 points or more depending on how many mistakes you might have. Below are steps to achieve 100+ points credit score increase:

1. Obtain a current copy of your credit report.

2. Identify negative entries on your credit reports.

3. Challenge late payments, inaccuracies, collections, and charge offs by using the sample letters that are located within the appendix. I prefer writing (snail mail) compared to online disputes because snail mail increases the chances of human interaction.

4. Optimize your credit utilization ratio. Keep it low, 30% and below.

5. Establish a solid payment history by paying all your bills on time, each month. Make payment arrangements when and if necessary, to avoid late payments and late fees.

6. Limit credit inquiries to your credit by not applying for many loans.

7. Build positive credit with a secured credit card by paying off the total amount that you spend within 25 days or less, if possible. Unsecured credit cards are also optional and should be paid the say way.

8. Become an authorized user on someone else's bank and / or credit account.

9. Consider asking someone who trusts you, to become a co-signer on a bank / credit account for you. Be sure to make the payments on time, each

month. This will also help you increase your credit score.

CHAPTER 2: FICO Score

Fair Isaac Corporation (FICO) is the company that develops and maintains the mathematical formula to calculate FICO Scores. FICO calculates your FICO Scores using information kept at the credit bureaus. Each credit bureau uses their own algorisms to determine credit scores.

You may decide to apply for a mortgage or home loan at various points in your life. A significant factor that banks and creditors consider before lending is your FICO ranking. (Williams, 2004). It is one of the most common instruments used in the U.S. to determine financial or creditworthiness. Therefore, you must know what a FICO score is, how it is calculated, and the factors affecting it so that you can fix it if needed and increase your chances of receiving loans with lower interest rates.

The said score is prepared by credit bureaus known as reporting agencies that collect information from past and current financial transactions and creditors' loans and measure your score based on certain factors. These considerations include your unpaid loan amounts, payment history, credit history, and new credits and credit forms, among others. Past and current financial credit conditions are analyzed, and the borrower's default risks or probability are measured. The score is a 3-digit numbers from 300 to

850. A high score indicates a greater potential and chance to remain in charge of your finances and maintain a healthy financial lifestyle, resulting in a higher likelihood of banks and creditors granting you credit.

However, having a low FICO score does not end your chances of having reasonable interest rates. You can still get higher scores by enhancing significant factors that influence it, such as your payment history, and reducing your unpaid debts for a start. Many factors will help you gain the most favorable ranking, pay attention to the specifics, and strengthen your current credit condition's critical areas.

Why Does FICO Exist?

A man named Fair Isaac developed the FICO score as a means of measuring scores to determine a person's financial lifestyle and activities. The term FICO score derives from the company name Fair Isaac Corporation, founded by the inventor. The word "score" is added as it is a method of evaluation used by the same company. It's basically the credit score used to decide who can or can't get a credit loan.

What Is A Tri-Merge Report?

This is a report and tool that businesses and other financial institutions use to determine an individual borrower's payment history. These companies are provided with different scores from reporting agencies or Bureau. The total score is the collection of scores from Experian, TransUnion, and Equifax, called the Tri-merge report.

Note: A tri-merge credit report does not have any information that does not already appear on your credit reports. You can also purchase the three reporters' copies. You can compare the reports to analyze your current position better and help you make informed decisions in the future.

Difference between a Tri-Merge Report and FICO?

It is easy for people to easily get misconstrued between a credit report and a tri-merge report, and rightly so because of some common aspect to both reports.

Your FICO score is only one aspect of your credit report. Potential lenders evaluate your entire credit report to determine whether you're an acceptable credit risk for a new mortgage, credit card, auto loan, or personal loan. Creditors report late payments and other derogatory account activity to credit reporting agencies. Positive actions, such as paying your credit card bill on time each month, appear on your credit report as well. The resulting entries either diminish or improve your FICO score.

A tri-merge is a 3-in-1 report that summarizes the information provided by the three bureaus. Lenders and individuals who pull your credit often prefer to review a tri-merge report rather than relying on just one Bureau and score. For example, mortgage lenders use the middle FICO score on a tri-merge report when qualifying you for a home loan.

CHAPTER 3: Tiers and Tradelines

A tradeline is a term used by credit reporting agencies to describe credit accounts displayed on the report. For each account you have, there's a different tradeline that includes creditor and debt details.

How Are Tradelines Placed on Credit?

Understanding how trading lines operate will give you a better understanding of how to read your credit report and what lenders can see when reviewing your credit.

Tiers and tradelines are the meat and potatoes of the credit bureaus. It is where most details that makes up your score is derived. One field to consider, mainly when you look at accounts with a delinquent background, is the timing of delinquency. Delinquencies can send your credit score into nosedive. There are 4 delinquency that I refer to. I will briefly explain each stage, but it important that you avoid delinquencies.

> **Stage 1**: a 30-day delinquency occurs when you have gone roughly 30 days, after the due date, without paying your bill/s. Typically, there's a grace period here and it would behove you to contact your lender and inform them of your late

payment, as there may be something they can do to help such as offer you a payment arrangement.

Stage 2: a 60-day delinquency occurs when you have gone roughly 60 days, after the due date, without paying your bill/s. Although your repayment window of options may be closing, the creditor may still be willing to work with you. Remember, communication is key. So, should you find yourself in this stage, try to pay any amount towards to balance, that is agreed upon between you and the creditor.

Stage 3: a 90-day delinquency occurs when you have gone roughly 90 days, after the due date, without paying your bill/s. This stage will most surely impact your credit score negatively because creditors are close to declaring your account uncollectable, which is a 'charge-off'. The creditor may still be willing to work with you, especially if you have been experiencing financial hardships. You may also consider a Debt Management Plan (contact NFCC.org), which could halt the late payment fees and allow you to pay off what is due in a fraction of the time.

Stage 4: a 120-180-day delinquency occurs when you have gone between 120 and 180 days, after the due date, without paying your bill/s. You account will most certainly be considered a 'charge-off' at this stage. At this stage, some states have the authority to garnish your pay check or file a judgement against you. Do not avoid the debt collectors as they may be able to provide a settlement (get it in writing, with a clause that states you will not be sued as long as you're making payments) for you. Once you are paid the debt, make sure your credit report reflects that.

Delinquent accounts could lead to a lien in stage 4. A lien is a legal tool creditor use to stake a claim to an asset you're using as debt collateral. Liens are used as a backup to help safeguard lenders' investments, but can also be used as a remedy for creditors to collect unsatisfied debts whereas a trade line is a record of activity for any type of credit extended to a borrower and reported to a credit reporting agency. A trade line is established on a borrower's credit report when a borrower is approved for credit. The trade line records all of the activity associated with an account.

Typically, the payment history showing the extent and severity of overdue payments will reverse the payment history from the balance date displayed on the report. This history is a crucial step to remember because the recency of late payments is key to creditors' decision-making process.

Another reason for evaluating trade lines is the volume and form of revolving credit. The tradeline segment is where you can get more information about your credit. It allows you to do more of a detailed analysis. It is important to note that only one tier can be placed on a report. This is an overall score for all items listed on the credit report.

How do Tiers Differ?

Below are six key sections of your FICO credit score.

Tier One

Tier 1 credit scores are usually considered to be scores ranging from 760 to 850. Since credit scores deal with ranges and not individual scores, the FICO score of 760 is basically the same as 850 and will give you the same rate as the score of 850.

Tier Two

Tier Two credit ratings usually range from 700 to 759. Any FICO score inside the two-tier range is still considered to be very good credit. Consumers with Tier 2 credit scores will usually receive an interest rate that is a step down from the top interest rate. Anyone with a credit score of two levels should have no trouble applying for credit or credit cards.

Tier Three

Tier 3 credit scores typically range from 660 to 699. Having a credit score falling within the range of 660 to 699 means is indicative of good credit. Tier three FICO ratings will usually have no trouble applying for loans or credit cards, but they will not earn the best interest rate.

Tier Four

Scores ranging from 620 to 659 qualify as tier four credit scores, also known as 'Average' credit. Like the above, Tier 4 credit scores will usually qualify someone for loans and credit cards, but financial institutions will take a much longer and more in-depth look at the person's financial history.

Tier Five

A credit score that falls between 580 and 619 will place a person in the five-tier credit score. People with a credit score between 580 and 619 are deemed "subprime" by lenders. Qualifying for a loan becomes difficult in the five-tier range, and many lenders require either a co-signor or collateral to approve a loan for someone with a five-tier credit score. Interest rates will also rise dramatically for anyone considered to be subprime.

Tier Six

According to Bankrate.com, Tier 6 is the lowest range which yields the lowest workable credit score that allows anyone to apply for a decent mortgage loan, but higher interest rate. Tier 6 credit scores range from 500 to 579. People with a tier six credit score would be qualified for a rock-bottom interest rate if they apply at all. Many banks will need collateral or a co-signor to approve loans at this tier.

Can Tiers and Tradelines Be Removed?

You can ask to remove a tradeline if fraudulently produced. Since it gets rid of an unwanted account that could have derogatory details attached to it, deleting a tradeline may be a positive thing for your credit. As the goal is the challenge and remove all inaccurate and derogatory details from your credit report.

Therefore, if the tradeline has useful information to boost your credit scores, removal could affect your scores. On the other hand, if your credit card account has a high use or payment history problem, it can raise your credit scores.

CHAPTER 4: Inquiries

If one applies for a loan and a lender requests a copy of the credit report – this request is recorded as an "inquiry" in the applicant's credit file. Basically, a credit inquiry is a credit check. An inquiry occurs when there is a legal request from a person or a company to see your credit report.

Landlords use credit reports if you apply to rent an apartment or home. To check your credit report and credit rating or FICO score, they ask for your social security information, birth date, and other information, and this is also an inquiry.

Another inquiry may be from your boss or someone you have sent a resume to, but they can only look at your credit report with your written permission. An inquiry may also take the form of unsolicited credit deals, such as credit card offers or home equity loan offers. These can come in the mail and are called "prescreening."

Credit inquiries arise while seeking credit. These inquiries will appear on your credit report and could potentially lower your score. They count against your FICO ranking, but only moderately. The effect inquiries on your credit score depending on what form of inquiry. Loans that typically require "rate-shopping," such as car loans or mortgages, may not weigh as heavily as other forms of inquiries.

There usually are two forms of inquiries — soft and hard-pull inquiries.

Soft pull inquiries: occur in the circumstances like; when a current creditor pulls your credit to review your financial situation, when you pull your credit report, or when a corporation purchases your details from any of the three credit reporting agencies. Soft pulls are essentially harmless and in no way affect your credit score.

Hard-pull inquires: In comparison, hard-pull inquiries occur when applying for a new credit cap, a new credit card, or request a loan application.

Can an Inquiry Be Removed?

Removing credit inquiries is a procedure you may want to consider doing from time to time to avoid wreaking havoc on your credit score. There are several explanations of why your credit report can include an inquiry. This could involve asking your credit card company to raise your credit limit, applying for a loan to purchase a house or vehicle, reacting to a credit offer in your mail, and others.

The key stages to remove credit inquiries are:

1. Find out which credit inquiries trigger problems. To do this, you need to view all three credit reports.

Upon arrival, check records and locate inquiries usually at the end. Identify which credit queries will be visible to your credit service. Some may be very obvious, while others may be a complete mystery, so please write them down.

2. Inquiry challenge (Please find sample letters within the appendix section of this book).

   This stage is achieved by submitting letters questioning any inquiry you have considered troublesome. Request proof of authorization and send each inquiry letter via Certified Mail Return Receipt-no signature needed. So you'll have a paper trail you can show to prove the actions you've taken.

3. Check and recheck your report once your completed steps 1 and 2 above. Be mindful that some creditors will provide you with inquiry documents, and others will not. For those who do, remember to check and recheck the paperwork to ensure you approved the inquiry. If there is any misunderstanding, you can write back and complain about any of your findings. It's relatively better for those who don't have the evidence since being unable to provide enough

proof would mean that they have no choice but to remove the inquiry.

Removing credit inquiries maybe a little hassling and can take some time. Nonetheless, it's something you really should take into account, as they will later cause you numerous unexpected problems.

How to dispute an error on your credit report

Dispute the information with the credit reporting company. If you identify an error on your credit report, you should start by disputing that information with the credit reporting company (Experian, Equifax, and / or TransUnion). You should explain in writing what you think is wrong, why, and include copies of documents that support your dispute. You can also use our instructions and template letter as a guide. If you mail a dispute, be sure to:

1. Provide your contact information including complete name, address, and telephone number.
2. Reference an account number or confirmation number, if available.
3. Identify each mistake, such as an account number for any account you may be disputing and reference it within the letter.
4. Explain why you are disputing the information.

5. Request that the information be removed or corrected.

6. Enclose a copy of the portion of your credit report that contains the disputed items and circle or highlight the disputed items. You should include copies (not originals) of documents that support your position.

7. You may choose to send your letter of dispute to credit reporting companies by certified mail and ask for a return receipt so that you will have a record that your letter was received. (Additional sample letters can be found within the appendix)

{Name}   {Credit Bureau: Name}
{Address}   {Credit Bureau: Address}
{Phone #}

{Date}

RE: Request for Investigation of Unauthorized Credit on my Account

Dear Sir/Ma'am,

I checked my credit report, which I acquired from your organization on { **insert date of report** } and I noticed a discrepancy. An Unauthorized credit inquiry has been made.

I contacted {**Inquiry source's name**}, who conducted the inquiry and asked them to remove their credit from my credit profile.

I request that you initiate an investigation into {**Inquiry source's name**} inquiry on my credit report to determine who exactly authorized the inquiry. If, once your investigation is complete, you find my allegation to be true, please remove the inquiry and send me an updated copy of my credit report at the address listed above.

If you find the inquiry refrenced above to be valid, please send me a description of the procedures used in your investigation within 15 business days of the completion of the investigation.

Thank you for your assistance in this matter.

{Signature}
{Printed Name}

CHAPTER 5: Chex Systems

While you may be familiar with the three major credit reporting agencies that look at your overall financial health and provide credit reports, you may or may not be aware of an agency that tracks your banking behavior.

The agency's name is ChexSystem. If you have ever had a bank to close check or savings account due to too many overdrafts or other problems with your account, you may have ended up with your name in the ChexSystem files.

Chex System is a consumer reporting bank account screening agency (CRA). It works behind the scenes of the financial system to help banks and financial institutions pre-screen new customers applying for bank accounts. Banks use ChexSystems to decide which customers, based on their previous behavior, may be at higher risk of misusing or misusing their bank accounts.

According to the National Consumer Law Center, over 80% of banks use a bank account screening CRA, like ChexSystems, to evaluate whether to approve customers for a new account. The ChexSystems Consumer Score is typically more useful to banks than it is to consumers. Unless you have had a history of serious problems with managing a bank account, you usually won't have to think about your ChexSystems report or ChexSystems score at all.

What Is Reported to Chex Systems?

To ensure that only financially responsible individuals open checking accounts at member institutions, these banks report on customers displaying poor financial management skills. The credit services and banks report to Chex systems when a customer's checking account is closed due to proven mismanagement. If done, the consumer would have a challenging time opening an account at any other financial institution partnered with Chex Systems for the next several years.

Since most financial institutions (banks) reject potential customers on file at Chex Systems, reporting may position a person at a severe disadvantage. But what, exactly, does it take to get a checking account closed and reported to Chex Systems in the first place? The answer the bank usually provides is "closed for a cause." Yet there are many ways that a customer can end up having his or her account terminated. This could be as a result of severe fraudulent transactions to excessive overdrafts. But note that policy can differ significantly between financial institutions. Depending on which bank is involved, cases where accounts are "closed for cause" may mean that you:

1. Are not or have not reimbursed their bank for overdraft fees.
2. Misused savings accounts, ATMs, or debit cards.
3. Provided misleading or incorrect information on the account.

However, while many reasons may contribute to account termination, banks are not always forthcoming due to the precise reason for terminating an account. This action can lead to some uncertainty, and a new account rejected.

How Can Chex Systems Be Disputed?

A Chex Systems report can be disputed if a financial institution unfairly puts you on their list. If a bank thinks you have written a check with insufficient money, closed an overdrawn bank account, or done something they do not like, they will report you to Chex Systems. Once your name is on their list, it would stay on your report for five years unless you take steps to get it resolved amicably.

If not deleted, you can add a comment to the item describing your side of the story. Write Chex Systems, asking them to include a customer statement and what you want to appear. It should be less than 100 words, cannot mention another person's name or company, and should be a concise description of why they should not count the report. When you apply for a bank account, and the bank pulls your Chex systems report, they will be able to read your statement, so think about what you'd like to say and the impression you want to give.

If you cannot obtain resolve with Chex Systems and are still having trouble opening a bank account, here is some good news for you. Some banks do not use Chex Systems! In that case, applying for an account with a bank that does not use Chex Systems could be the easiest solution to establishing a banking savings and or checking account.

CHAPTER 6: The Consumer Financial Protection Bureau

The Consumer Financial Protection Bureau was created as part of the 2010 Consumer Protection Act to protect families from unethical practices in banking, lending, and personal credit industries. Its goal is to level the landscape for consumer financial goods and services for American families.

The agency has authority-making and supervisory powers, and to restore the fragmented consumer credit system, it uses a combination of technology and consumer education to fulfil its mandate.

The Consumer Financial Protection Bureau (CFPB) is the culmination of decades-longest reform of the financial system and puts all consumer credit firms under one watch, including financial goods and services like;

➢ Credit cards

➢ Mortgages

➢ Payday loans

➢ Private Student loans

Why Do Consumer Financial Protection Bureaus Exist?

The Bureau is responsible for enforcing existing banking and credit laws. They suggest new legislation that can affect everything from credit rules and regulations to how banks and creditors can solicit customers for its credit products and the remedies consumers have when they fall victim to predatory lending practices. The Bureau also supervises non-auto dealer loans.

Who Does the Consumer Financial Protection Bureau Support?

The Consumer Financial Protection Bureau (CFPB) was created in the wake of the financial crisis to stand up for consumers and make sure they are treated fairly in the consumer financial marketplace. Helping consumers help themselves with tools, and financial education is core to the Bureau's mission. Consumers can contact the CFPB to get help if they have a financial product or service problem. The CFPB also works directly with consumers to help avoid financial problems by giving them the resources they need to better understand products or financial decisions.

The Bureau aims to provide consumers with the tools they need to plan for the future and make financial choices that support their financial well-being.

Since the Bureau launched in July 2011, it has handled more than 1,242,800 complaints.

As of July 1, 2017, these include:

- ➤ 338,700 debt collection complaints
- ➤ 285,200 mortgage complaints
- ➤ 218,100 credit reporting complaints
- ➤ 125,100 credit card complaints
- ➤ 120,900 bank account and services complaints
- ➤ 48,300 student loan complaints
- ➤ 32,700 vehicle loan or lease complaints
- ➤ 22,900 personal loan complaints
- ➤ 18,200 payday loan complaints
- ➤ 14,800 money transfer or service or virtual currency complaints
- ➤ 7,300 prepaid card complaints

What Is a 609 Dispute Letter?

Section 609 refers to a section of the Fair Credit Reporting Act (FCRA) that addresses your rights to request copies of your own credit reports and associated information that appears on your credit reports. Section 609, oddly enough, doesn't have anything to do with your right to dispute information on your credit reports or a credit reporting agency's obligation to perform investigations into your disputes.

The 609 Dispute Letter theory is if you ask the credit bureaus for information they clearly cannot produce as part of your dispute letter, like the original signed copies of your credit applications or the cashed checks used for bill payment, then they would have to remove the disputed item because it's unverifiable.

Sample of a 609 Letter

Sample 609 Letter

Name
Address
Phone Number
Account # (if available)

Name of Company/Point Person
Relevant Department
Address

Date

Dear [Name of credit reporting agency],

I am writing to exercise my right to question the validity of the debt your agency claims I owe, pursuant to the Fair Credit Reporting Act (FCRA).

As stated in Section 609 of the FCRA, (2) (E): A consumer reporting agency is not required to remove accurate derogatory information from a consumer's file unless the information is outdated under Section 609 or cannot be verified.

As is my right, I am requesting verification of the following items:

[List any/all items you're looking to dispute, including the account name(s) and number(s) as listed on your credit report]

Additionally, I have highlighted these items on the attached copy of the credit report I received.

I request that all future correspondence be done through the mail or email. As stated in the FCRA, you are required to respond to my dispute within 30 days of receipt of this letter. If you fail to offer a response, all disputed information must be deleted.

Thank you for your prompt attention to this matter.

Sincerely

[Your signature]
[Your name]

CHAPTER 7: The Fair Credit Reporting Act

The U.S. government enacted a law called the Fair Credit Reporting Act (FCRA). This law governs what our credit reports should report, who can access our credit history, and much, much more.

The federal Fair Credit Reporting Act (FCRA) promotes the accuracy, fairness, and privacy of information in consumer reporting agencies' files. ("Summary of Your Rights Under the Fair Credit Reporting Act, CFPB," 2015)

The legislation requires customers to see what's included in their credit report. Previously, credit reporting agencies shared customer credit history with financial institutions, putting customers entirely out of the loop. The legislation provides greater clarity about what is said about us as customers, enabling us to receive credit reports.

The Fair Credit Reporting Act ("FCRA") applies to companies known as consumer reporting agencies or CRAs. They compile and sell consumer reports containing consumer information used or expected to be used for credit, employment, insurance, housing, or other similar decisions about consumers' eligibility for certain benefits and transactions. CRAs include credit bureaus, background screening companies, tenant screening companies, and check verification services. Credit reports, credit scores, and employment background screening reports are all types of consumer reports. CRAs must implement reasonable procedures to ensure maximum accuracy of consumer reports and provide consumers with access to their information, along with the ability to correct any errors. The FCRA also requires furnishers, those companies that regularly provide information about their customers to CRAs, to have procedures to ensure that the information they are reporting is accurate and complete and investigate consumer disputes about the accuracy of the information provided to CRAs.

Also, FCRA is very clear who can read our reports and who can't. FCRA allows an individual to have a clear permissible intent before obtaining the right to pull your credit history.

As referenced previously, the below is a list of possible organizations that can pull your credit report under some circumstances:

Lenders: Whenever you apply for a loan, you give the potential lender or credit card company legal permission to pull your credit report.

Utility companies: Utility providers and cell phone companies run a credit check on you when you apply for a new service. They are extending you a monthly service;

they want to make sure you have a positive history of paying back your debts.

Employers, Landlords, and Insurance Companies: All may be able to check your credit if you apply for a job, an apartment, or a new insurance policy.

A court of law: The court can also issue a subpoena for your credit history if relevant to a lawsuit. Also, a child support agency has the right to pull a parent's credit report to establish the ability to make child support payments

Personal Request: Remember that you have the right to review your credit report at any time. There is never a penalty because of pulling your report.

The FCRA: The FCRA also entitles us to accurate credit reports. This means that if there are errors or fraud in your report, the credit bureaus and your creditors have a legal responsibility to remove the mistakes once you alert them. You are legally entitled to report inaccurate information on your report and receive a response from the bureaus (within 30-45 days) addressing your concern.

What Is Credit History?

The main component of your financial life is your credit history. Your credit history is a historical reference to how you repay your debts. You construct a credit history over time.

As you may have realized by now, damaging your credit history is easy to do, if you become delinquent. Pay a few bills for the past 30 days, neglect debt collectors, or even co-sign for anyone else who is careless with their bills, and you've started to affect your credit adversely. Many times, these errors take a few months to show on your credit report, but it is incumbent upon you to understand the circumstances of any delinquent accounts.

Details and credit scores start decent. Typically, seven (7) years is the length of time a credit report indicates a negative item, such a lien, but it is more nuanced. Below you will find references to how long some items may remain on your credit report.

Insolvency: If you have applied for bankruptcy, your credit history will be listed after ten (10) years.

Tax lines: If you were liable for government taxes, the details would remain on the credit history report for seven (7) years from the payment date.

Default loan: If you default to the U.S. government or a subsidized student loan, the loan details will be reported seven (7) years after the guarantor's intervention.

Legal suits: Judgments against you in a loan case may be reported for seven (7) years or for the limitation's status duration, whichever is longer.

CONCLUSION

Too many people do not know their credit score, have no credit, don't know what's on their credit report, or may not be aware of what a FICO score means. Increasing your credit score is something that we should all work on doing.

The main factors in a FICO score are:

1. Payment History consists of 35% of your score.
2. Credit Balances makes up 30% of your score.
3. Length of Credit History makes up 15% of your score.
4. New Credit makes up 10% of your score.
5. A mixture of various credit accounts makes up the remaining 10% of your score.

I would like to quickly reference VantageScore here. The VantageScore is a newer credit scoring model which was created by Experian, TransUnion, and Equifax; and launched in 2006. FICO launched in 1989.

the VantageScore is not widely used as the FICO, it is becoming more popular. Your VantageScore can be based upon any of the three credit reports but is used slightly different in weighting factors compared to FICO.

The main factors in a VantageScore are:

1. Payment History consists of 40% of your score.

2. Length and Types of credit makes up 21% of your score.

3. Credit Utilization consists of 20% of your score.

4. Credit Balances makes up 11% of your score.

5. Recent Credit Applications makes up 5% of your score.

6. Available Credit consists of 3% of your credit score.

FICO and VantageScore Categories	FICO Score Range	VantageScore Range
Excellent	800-850	780-850
Very Good / Good	740-799	661-780
Good / Fair	670-739	601-660
Fair / Poor	580-669	500-600
Very Poor	300-579	300-499

You should consider tracking your FICO and VantageScore. As shown in the table above, the FICO and VantageScore both range from 300 points to 850 points. Equipped with your credit scores, you will be better able to make wise and long-term financial decisions.

Sharing the fundamentals of budgeting will educate us all and put us on a path towards having very good to excellent credit. Everyone should know the basics of building good credit.

Here are four things that can be applied to your current budget that will help you improve your credit over time and help put you in a better place financially.

1. **Prioritizing debt payoff**

Put as much as you can towards debt repayment of the bills that are considered top priority. Accordingly, list bills in order of relevance and priority and designate the exact dollar amount to be paid to said bill monthly. Develop and use a checklist for each month and check off each item once paid. Hold yourself accountable. Even doing so temporarily to get your utilization below 30% is worth the effort.

2. **Make all your payments on time**

Make sure you have the financial resources to make all your payments when they are due. As mentioned previously, avoid paying bills late because it could lead to a negative impact to your credit score. Here are some key ways to avoid late payments: learn your billing cycle, sign up for bill reminders, allow a cushion of time to allow your payment to arrive, and create a bill paying location in your home where you sit and pay bills.

3. **Make multiple credit card payments every month**

If you get paid twice a month or weekly, schedule credit card payments for the following business day. This will help keep your balances low and keep you from overspending, which is win-win! Depending upon how your credit card issuer calculates finance charges, making multiple monthly payments could also help you save on interest. Making multiple monthly payments ensures that you should not have to worry about late payments, considering that you make the first monthly payment on or before the due date.

4. **Put money in savings for emergencies**

Start setting aside $50-100 every month strictly for emergency savings. A preferred way to do this is to prioritize debt repayment until your utilization is below 30% while saving for emergencies. Once your debt is below that ratio, you can throw additional money into your emergency savings account.

In the United States, less than 50% of Americans have obtained their free credit report this year, which everyone is entitled to. On top of that, "the average FICO score in America is 691. According to FINRA Investor Education Foundation, Sallie Mae, TransUnion, Experion, roughly 2% of undergraduate students have no credit history.

These facts prove that Americans need to devote time to learning more about their budgeting, money management, and finance circumstance.

Finance encompasses banking, leverage or debt, credit, capital markets, money, investments, and the creation and oversight of financial systems. Financial planning involves analyzing the current financial position of individuals to formulate strategies for future needs within financial constraints. Personal finance is specific to every individual's situation and activity; therefore, financial strategies depend largely on the person's earnings, living requirements, goals, and desires.

Many individuals save for retirement, for example, which requires saving or investing enough money during their employment years to fund their long-term plans. This type of financial management decision falls under personal finance.

A credit score is what lenders look at and base their decisions upon. For a credit card company, bank, or loan company to loan consumers money, they need to know the risk involved. The credit bureaus provide lenders with a consumer credit score, which helps a loan companies evaluate the risk involved with loaning someone money.

Here are some friendly reminders of what you should consider doing to see an increase of 100+ points. To increase your credit score with that margin in 12 months or less, consumers will need to follow these rules.

1. Keep your credit card balances low

If you can keep your credit card balances below 30% of your credit limit, this will help build good credit. In other words, don't max out your credit cards because this can lower your credit score. If you already have maxed out credit cards and have fallen behind on your accounts, then debt settlement can help you settle your debts, get them paid off, and allow you to start fresh.

2. Pay off credit cards balances monthly

This is an excellent habit to inculcate. If you can do this, it will help you immensely in building good to excellent credit. You will have healthy creditworthiness. However, as mentioned in rule one, if you accumulate a balance on your cards, keep your balance below 30% of your limit to build credit.

3. Have a good mixture of accounts

Having a good mixture of accounts, including revolving credit and installment loans like car payments or mortgage payments, is beneficial in some ways. Lenders like to see that you have an excellent mixture of accounts on your credit report that you are paying responsibly on.

It is never too late to start building your credit. Bad credit happens, but that does not mean that you cannot restart. Personal loans are the opportunity that will help build a good credit history. If you refrain from making any further mistakes with bad credit personal loans, it will positively affect your credit report. However, credit rebuilding does not take place overnight. With time and a little patience, you will be proud of your efforts and your credit score.

GLOSSARY

Affordable - that which you have the financial means for.

Authorization - the act of conferring legality or sanction or formal warrant; official permission or approval; the power or right to give orders or make decisions.

Bankruptcy - a legal process intended to insure equality among the creditors of a corporation declared to be insolvent; inability to discharge all your debts as they come due.

Borrower - someone who receives something on the promise to return it or its equivalent.

Bureau - an administrative unit of government.

Consolidation - the act of combining into an integral whole.

Counselling - direction or advice towards a decision for a course of action.

Credibility - the quality of being believable or trustworthy.

Credit - arrangement for deferred payment for goods and services; money available for a client to borrow; an accounting entry acknowledging income or capital items; approval.

Creditworthiness - trustworthiness with money as based on a person's credit history, a general qualification for borrowing.

Delinquent - past due; not paid at the scheduled time; persistently bad; guilty of a minor misdeed; failing in what duty requires; noun a young offender.

Derogatory - expressive of low opinion.

Dispute - coming into conflict with; a disagreement or argument about something important.

Eligible - qualified for or allowed or worthy of being chosen.

Fraudulently - in a dishonest and fraudulent manner.

History - the aggregate of past events; the continuum of events occurring in succession leading from the past to the present and even into the future.

Identity - the distinct personality of an individual regarded as a persisting entity; exact sameness; the individual characteristics by which a thing or person is recognized or known.

Insurance - promise of reimbursement in the case of loss; paid to people or companies so concerned about hazards that they have made prepayments to an insurance company; protection against future loss.

Lending - disposing of money or property with the expectation that the same thing (or an equivalent) will be returned.

Lien - the right to take another's property if an obligation is not discharged.

Mortgage - a conditional conveyance of property as security for the repayment of a loan.

Policy - a plan of action adopted by an individual or social group.

Rating - an appraisal of the value of something.

Receipt - an acknowledgment (usually tangible) that payment has been made; the act of receiving; mark or stamp as paid.

Strategy - the branch of military science dealing with military command and the planning and conduct of a war; an elaborate and systematic plan of action.

Struggling - engaged in a struggle to overcome especially poverty or obscurity.

Transactions – the instance of buying or selling something.

REFERENCES

1. Consumer Financial Protection Bureau: Helping consumers help themselves–JULY 2017 (www.consumerfinance.gov.)

2. https://www.creditknocks.com/what-is-equifax/

3. Leonard, R., and Lamb, A., 2002. *Credit Repair*. 6th ed. Berkely: Delta Printing Solutions, INC.

4. PUBLICATION: Daily Herald (Arlington Heights, IL), June 25, 2011.

5. PUBLICATION: St. Joseph News-Press, October 29, 2012.

6. PUBLICATION: Daily Herald (Arlington Heights, IL), June 25, 2011.

7. PUBLICATION: St. Joseph News-Press, October 29, 2012.

8. Sample Letter for Disputing Errors on Your Credit Report. (2013). *FTC*.

9. See Credit Reports and Scores, CFPB, https://www.consumerfinance.gov/consumer-tools/credit-reportsand-scores

10. Summary of Your Rights Under the Fair Credit Reporting Act, CFPB. (2015). from http://files.consumerfinance.gov

11. Williams, B. (2004). *Debt for Sale: A Social History of Credit Trap*. University of Pennsylvania Press.

APPENDIX: Sample Letters

{Name}   {Credit Bureau: Name}
{Address}   {Credit Bureau: Address}
{Phone #}

{Date}

RE: Request for Investigation of Unauthorized Credit on my Account
Dear Sir/Ma'am,

I checked my credit report, which I acquired from your organization on **{ insert date of report }** and I noticed a discrepancy. An Unauthorized credit inquiry has been made.

I contacted **{Inquiry source's name}**, who conducted the inquiry and asked them to remove their credit from my credit profile.

I request that you initiate an investigation into **{Inquiry source's name}** inquiry on my credit report to determine who exactly authorized the inquiry. If, once your investigation is complete, you find my allegation to be true, please remove the inquiry and send me an updated copy of my credit report at the address listed above.

If you find the inquiry refrenced above to be valid, please send me a description of the procedures used in your investigation within 15 business days of the completion of the investigation.

Thank you for your assistance in this matter.

{Signature}
{Printed Name}

{Name}   {Credit Bureau: Name}
{Address}   {Credit Bureau: Address}
{Phone #}

{Date}

RE: Request Investigation of Credit Inquiry

Dear Sir/Ma'am,

After reviewing my credit report from [insert report bureau], I have noticed that the report shows [insert number] credit inquires that I did not authorize.

On June 19th, 2017, Company ABC issued an inquiry. I could not have authorized the inquiry as I was undergoing surgery at the time. Please see attached documents for verification.

Please investigate and remove these inquiries as quickly as possible. Shortly, I will be applying for a car loan, and it is important that my credit score accurately reflects my credit standing.

If you come across any evidence that counters my claim, please send me a copy.

Thank you for your diligence in looking into this issue.

Sincerely,

[Printed Name and Signature]

{Name}   {Credit Bureau: Name}
{Address}   {Credit Bureau: Address}
{Phone #}

{Date}

RE: Letter to Remove Incorrect Names and Old Phone Numbers

Dear Sir/Ma'am,

This letter is to formally request that you remove inaccurate information from my credit report. This inaccurate information has affected my chances of getting loans and credit. For your convenience, I am sending you the proof that the items are inaccurate in case you need to verify them before removing them.

I hereby request that you make these changes within 30 business days to avoid violating the FCRA. Please send me a copy of my credit report's changed details once you have made the changes.

Sincerely,

Signature of Sender
Sender's Name Printed

SAMPLE LETTER TO REMOVE OLD ADDRESS

{Name}   {Credit Bureau: Name}
{Address}   {Credit Bureau: Address}
{Phone #}

{Date}

RE: Request For Change of Address(Account Number if Applicable)

Dear Sir/Ma'am,

This is to inform you that I am changing my address as I move to a new residence on DATE. I would like you to change my address on your records and send any communications to the new address.

My current address is above, and my new address is:

New Address
City, State, Zip Code

Please send me confirmation that you have changed my address on your records. My email Name@email.com and my mobile phone number 555-123-4567, will not change.

Thank you for attending to this matter immediately.

Signature of Sender
Sender's Name Printed

Sample Letter for Disputing Billing Errors

[Date]

[Your Name]   [Name of Creditor]
[Your Address]   [Billing Inquiries]
[Your City, State, Zip Code]   [Address]
[Your Account Number]   [City, State, Zip Code]

Dear Sir or Madam:

I am writing to dispute a billing error in the amount of [$_____] on my account. The amount is inaccurate because [describe the problem]. I am requesting that the error be corrected, that any finance and other charges related to the disputed amount be credited as well, and that I receive an accurate statement.

Enclosed are copies of [use this sentence to describe any information you are enclosing, like sales slips or payment records] supporting my position. Please investigate this matter and correct the billing error as soon as possible.

Sincerely,

[Your name]

{Name}   {Credit Bureau: Name}
{Address}   {Credit Bureau: Address}
{Phone #}

{Date}

RE: Letter to Remove Items that were Removed and Placed Back on Report

Dear Sir/Ma'am,

After reviewing my credit report from [insert report bureau], I have noticed that the report shows [insert number] items that have been removed prior to this new credit report but somehow found itself back to this new credit report.

Please investigate and remove these items as quickly as possible. Shortly, I will be applying for a student loan, and it is important that my credit score accurately reflects my credit standing.

If you come across any evidence that counters my claim, please send me a copy.

Thank you for your diligence in looking into this issue.

Sincerely,

[Printed Name and Signature]

SAMPLE LETTER TO REMOVE TAX LIENS

Taxpayer Name:
SSN:
Street Address
City, State, Zip Code
Tax Period:
Tax Form: 10916(c)
To Whom It May Concern:

I am writing to request that you send written confirmation of the Withdrawal of a Federal Tax Lien to the following parties:

Experian National Consumer Assistance Center
P.O. Box 4500
Allen, TX 75013

TransUnion Consumer Relations
P.O. Box 2000
Chester, PA 19016-2000

Equifax Credit Information Services, LLC
P.O. Box 740241
Atlanta, GA 30374

I have attached a copy of Form 10916(c) Withdrawal of Filed Notice of Federal Tax Lien. This form indicates that the IRS withdrew the Federal Tax Lien. My records show that the tax lien is still on my credit report. Please send a copy of form 10916(C) and a request to remove the Federal Tax Lien to the credit bureaus above. You can reach me by phone at (###) ###-####.

Many thanks for your attention to this matter.

Sincerely,
Your Name
Attached: Form 10916(c)

Sample Letter to Remove Items that Resulted from Identity Theft

{Name}   {Credit Bureau: Name}
{Address}   {Credit Bureau: Address}
{Phone #}

{Date}

RE: Letter to Remove Items that Resulted from Identity Theft

Dear Sir/Ma'am,

I am a victim of identity theft. The information listed below, which appears on my credit report, does not relate to any transaction(s) that I have made. It is the result of identity theft.

[Identity item(s) resulting from the identity theft that should be blocked, by the name of the source, such as the credit card issuer or bank, and type of item, such as credit account, checking account, etc.]

Please block this information from my credit report, pursuant to section 605B of the Fair Credit Reporting Act, and send the required notifications to all furnishers of this information.

Find attached the following documents for your perusal.

[List what you are enclosing]

I appreciate your prompt attention to this matter and await your reply.

Sincerely,

[Your Name]

Stay Tuned for Volume 2

Do you desire to start a business, but not sure of how or where you may establish start-up capital? Would you like to get the credit and financing you need for your existing business? Would you like to know how to establish a credit score for your business?

Boosted: The Vital Credit, Budget & Financial Improver How-To Manual for Normal People, Volume 2 will address these questions and much more.

Please continue to make your credit a priority!!!

Stay abreast of updates! Click here to give permission to receive occasional emails or use the actual link below.

https://app.getresponse.com/site2/akarmstrong04?u=wfvcR &webforms_id=Bp9sG

www.ingramcontent.com/pod-product-compliance
Lightning Source LLC
Chambersburg PA
CBHW070945210326
41520CB00021B/7057